Students use cutouts provided in the book to work out math problems. Mathematical thinking skills are developed through concrete experience.

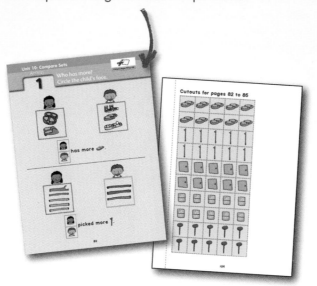

Some activities require the use of standard manipulatives and other materials. The materials and additional information required are indicated by the Toolbox and Notes.

Written exercises that focus on **repetition** ensure the reinforcement of mathematics facts and concepts.

A **variety of activities** such as games and practical tasks help to engage students in the revision of mathematical concepts. The activities in each unit are carefully sequenced for **progression in level of difficulty**.

© 2008 Marshall Cavendish International (Singapore) Private Limited

Published by Marshall Cavendish Education
An imprint of Marshall Cavendish International (Singapore) Private Limited
Times Centre, 1 New Industrial Road, Singapore 536196
Customer Service Hotline: (65) 6411 0820
E-mail: tmesales@sg.marshallcavendish.com
Website: www.marshallcavendish.com/education

Marshall Cavendish Corporation
99 White Plains Road
Tarrytown, NY 10591
U.S.A.
Tel: (1-914) 332 8888
Fax: (1-914) 332 8882
E-mail: mcc@marshallcavendish.com
Website: www.marshallcavendish.com

First published 2008
Reprinted 2009, 2010, 2011 (twice), 2012 (twice)

Marshall Cavendish is a trademark of Times Publishing Limited.

Earlybird Kindergarten Mathematics (Standards Edition) Activity Book A
ISBN 978-0-7614-7017-5

Printed in Singapore by Times Printers, www.timesprinters.com

SingaporeMath.com Inc®
Distributed by
SingaporeMath.com Inc
404 Beavercreek Road #225
Oregon City, OR 97045
U.S.A.
Website: www.singaporemath.com

CONTENTS

Blank

1

Match.

Cutouts: Page 93

Match the children to their clothes.

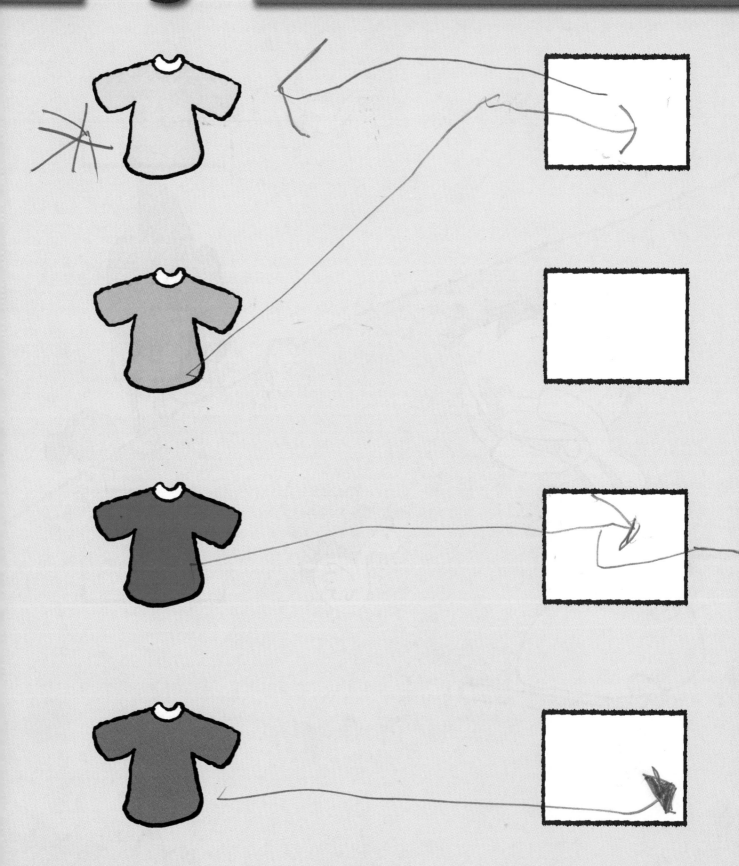

Match the children to their clothes.

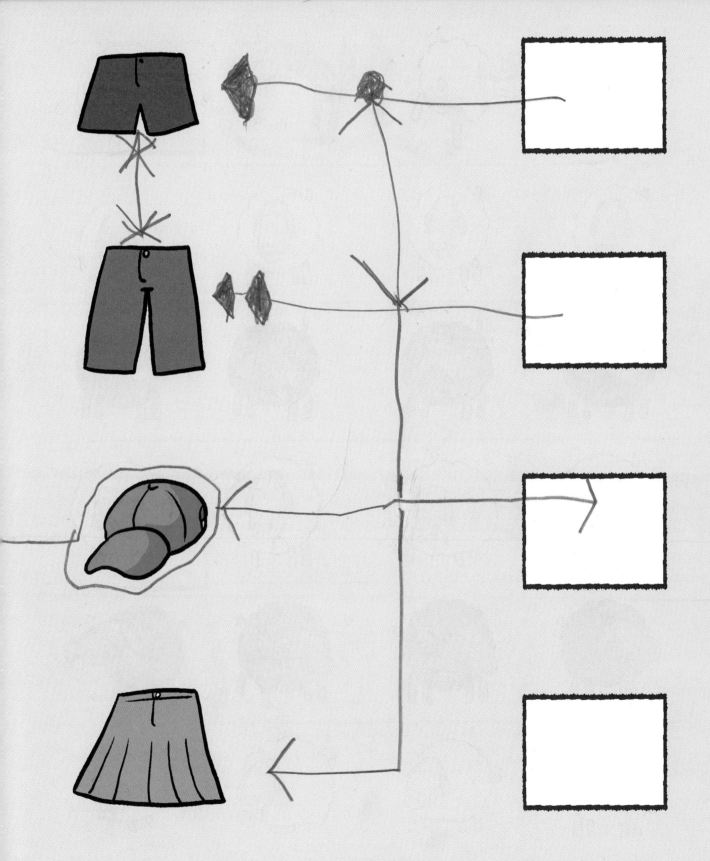

Circle the different one.

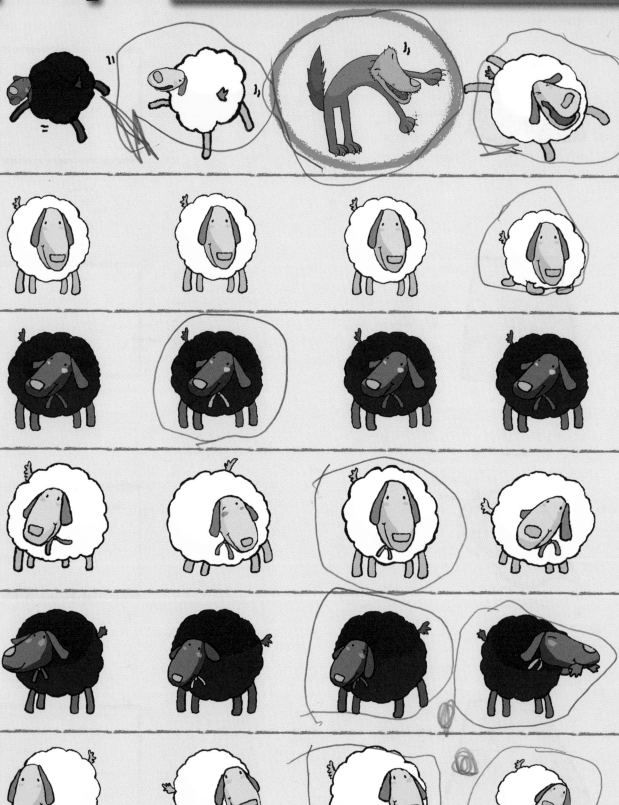

5

Put the sheep into groups.

Cutouts: Page 93

White sheep	Black sheep

Red ribbons	Blue ribbons

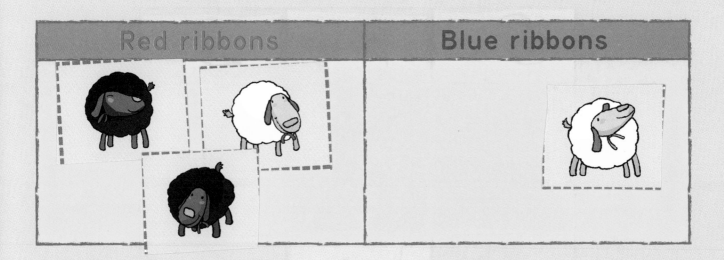

Small sheep	Big sheep

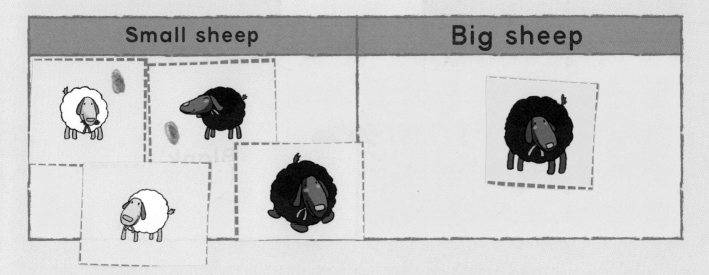

1 Count the bags.
Paste the cutouts.

Cutouts: Page 95

Baa, baa, black sheep
Have you any wool?

Yes, sir! Yes, sir! ...

4 bags full

�134 bags full

Count the bags.
Write the numbers.

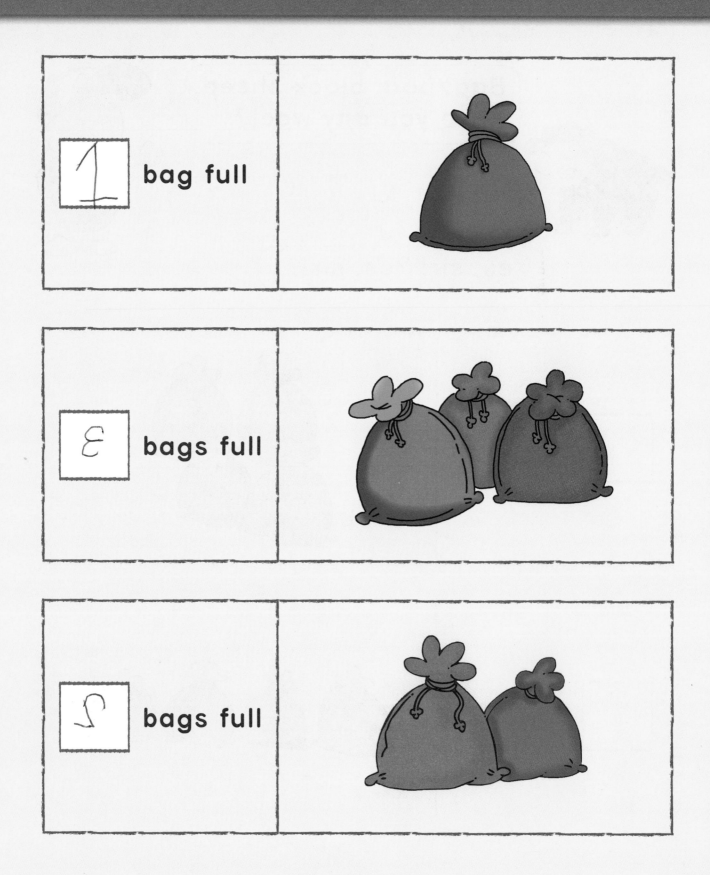

1 bag full

3 bags full

2 bags full

10

3

**Trace and write the numbers.
Color the bags.**

2 bags are blue.

2 2 2

1 bag is blue.

1

3 bags are blue.

3

Trace and write the numbers.
Color the bags.

4 bags are blue.

4

5 bags are blue.

5

2 bags are blue.

2

Paste the cutouts.
Trace and write the numbers.

Cutouts: Page 95

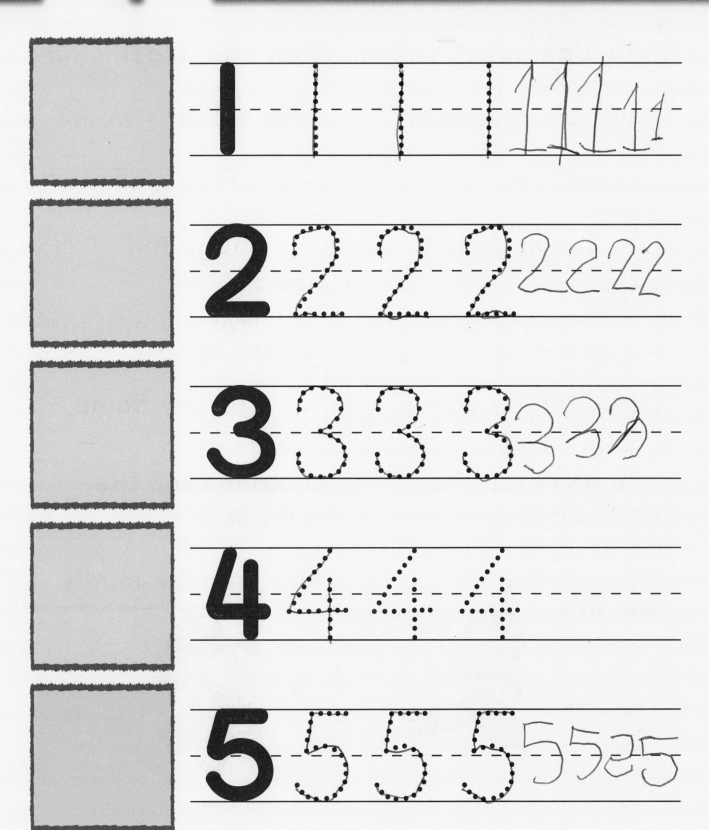

5

Listen to the rhyme.
Write the numbers.

Baa, baa, black sheep

Have you any wool?

Yes, sir! Yes, sir!

 bags full.

 for my master,

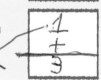 for my dame,

And none for the
little boy

Who lives down
the lane.

Baa, baa, black sheep

Have you any wool?

Yes, sir! Yes, sir!

☐ bags full.

☐ for my master,

☐ for my dame,

And none for the
little boy

Who cries so loudly.

Note: You may vary the numbers for each rhyme. The total number of bags in each rhyme should not exceed 5.

14

Baa, baa, black sheep

Have you any wool?

Yes, sir! Yes, sir!

☐ bags full.

☐ for my master,

☐ for my dame,

And none for the
little girl

Who smiles happily.

Baa, baa, black sheep

Have you any wool?

Yes, sir! Yes, sir!

☐ bags full.

☐ for my master,

☐ for my dame,

And none for the
little girl

Who counts correctly.

1

Read the numbers.
Paste the cutouts.

Cutouts: Page 95

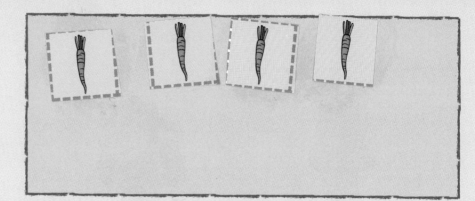

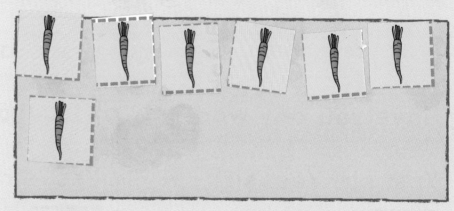

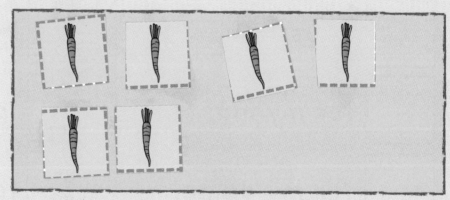

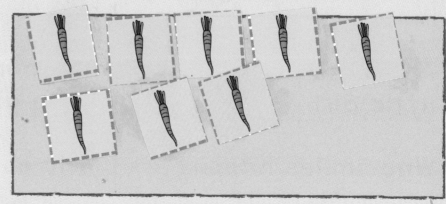

2

Count and match.

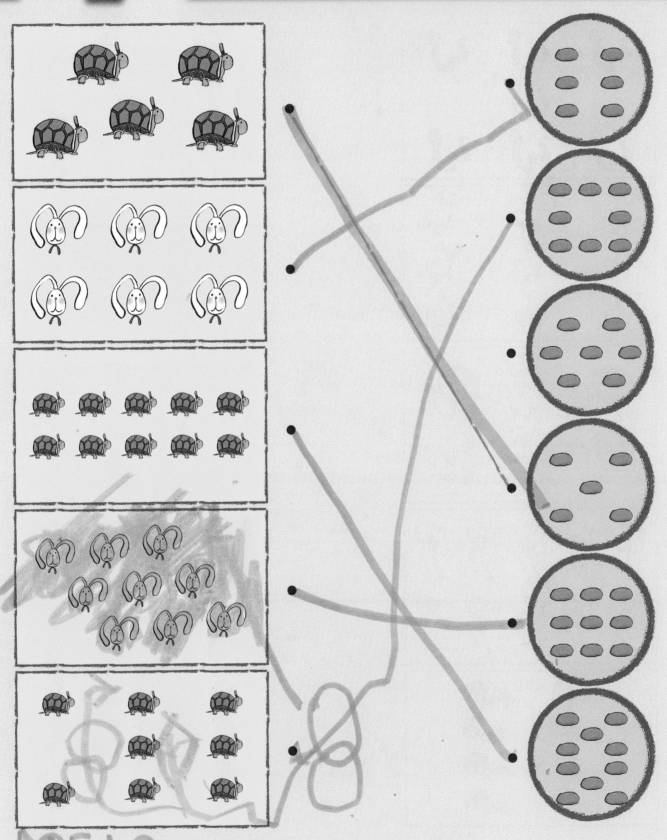

Count and match.

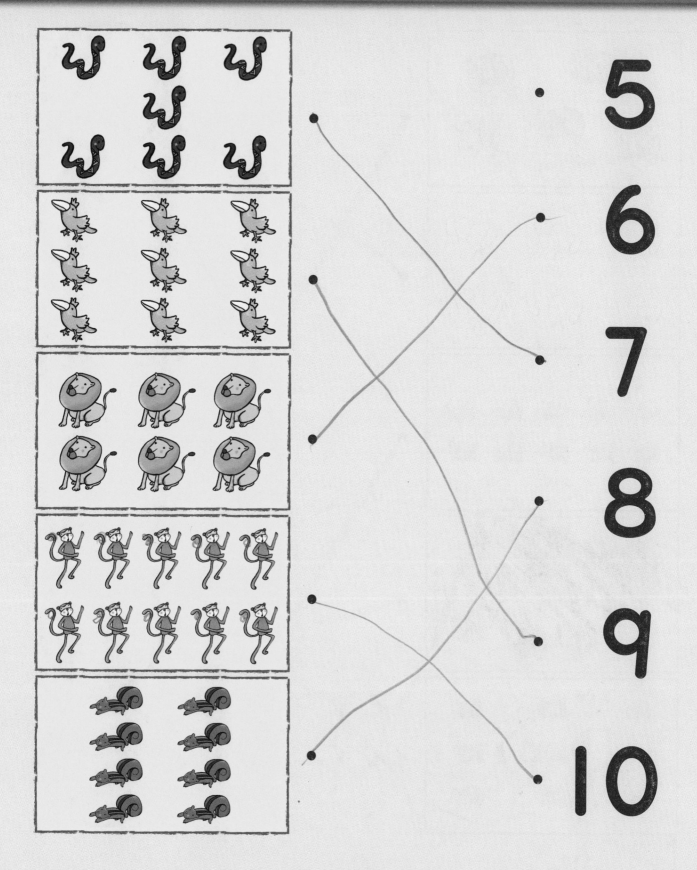

Count and match.

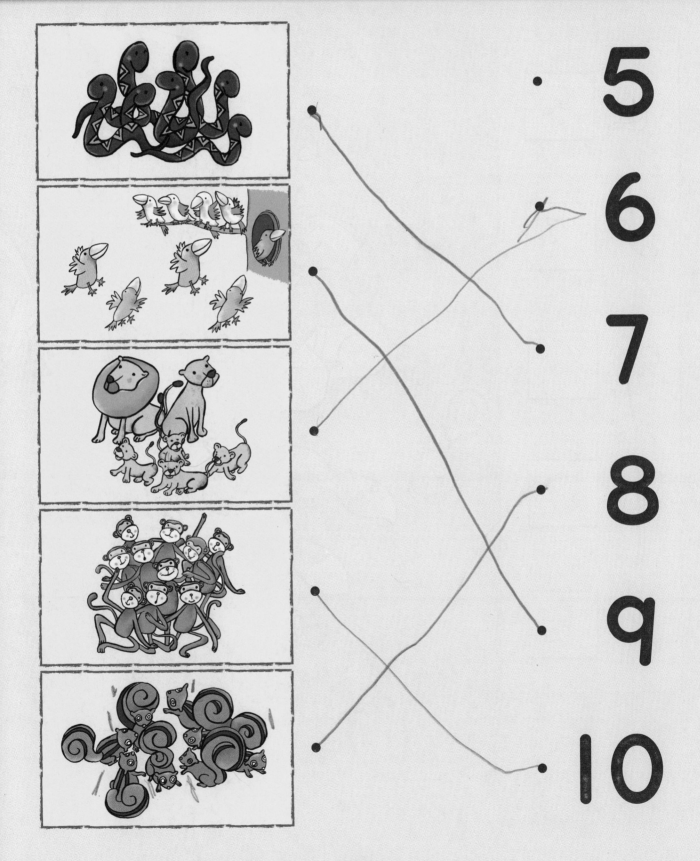

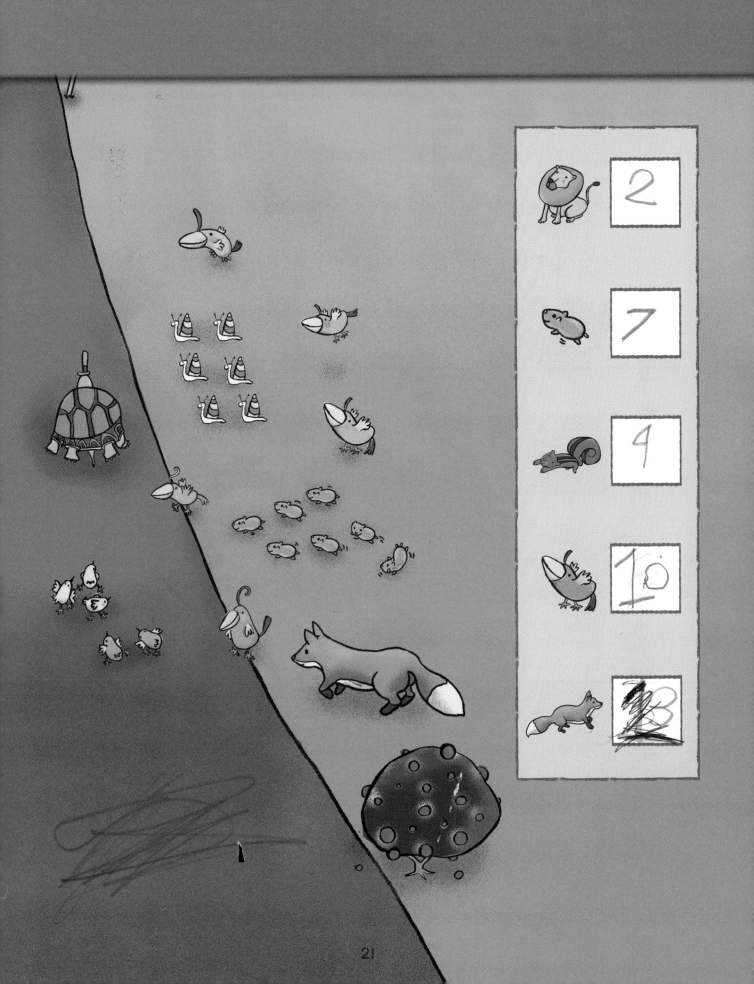

Activity 4

Count the carrots.
Write the numbers.

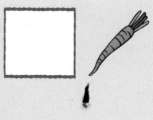

Count the carrots.
Write the numbers.

Activity

5 Count.

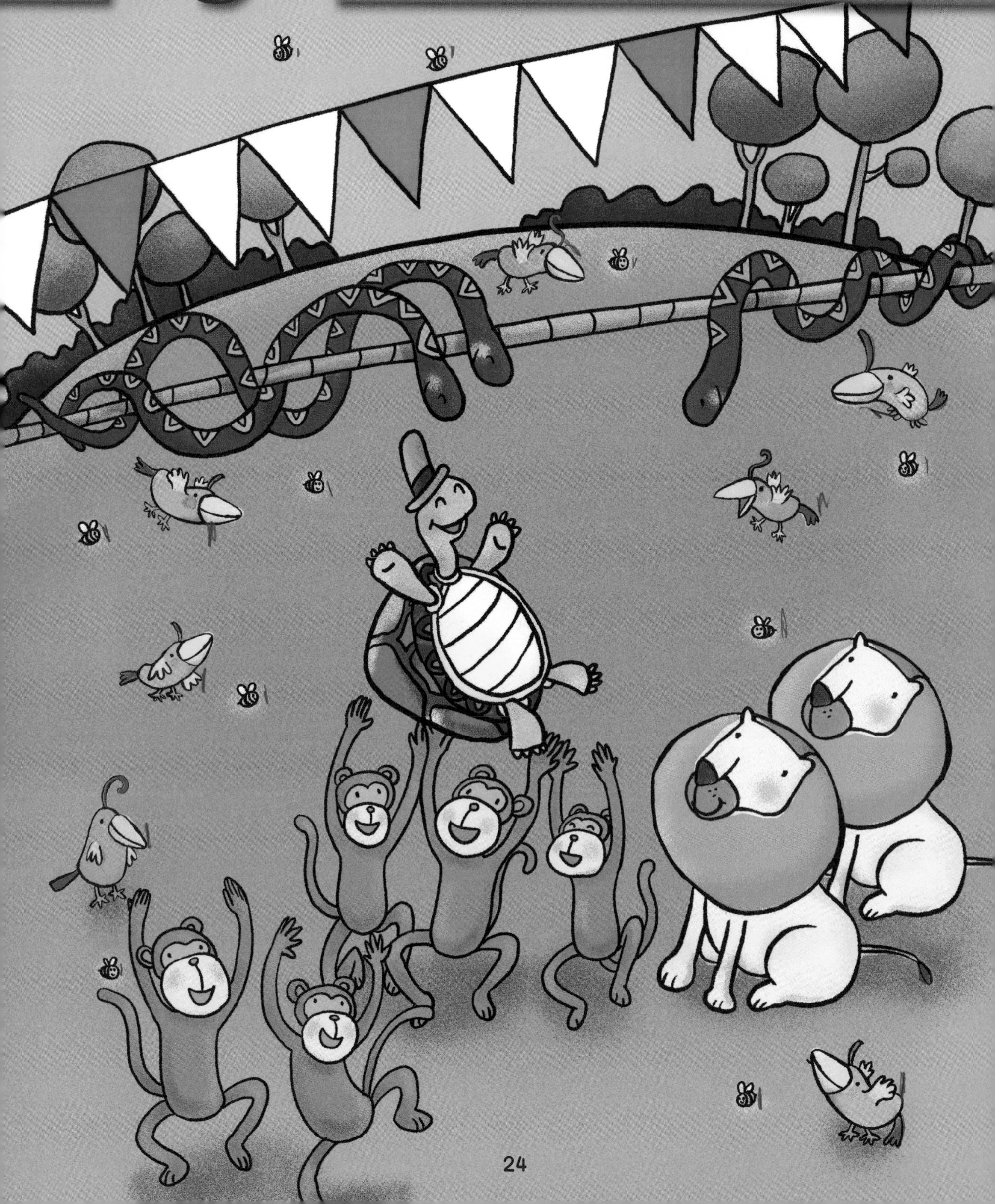

Write the numbers.

5 5 5

2

40

3

7

25

1

**Listen to the rhyme.
Tape the cutouts in order.**

Cutouts: Pages 97 and 99

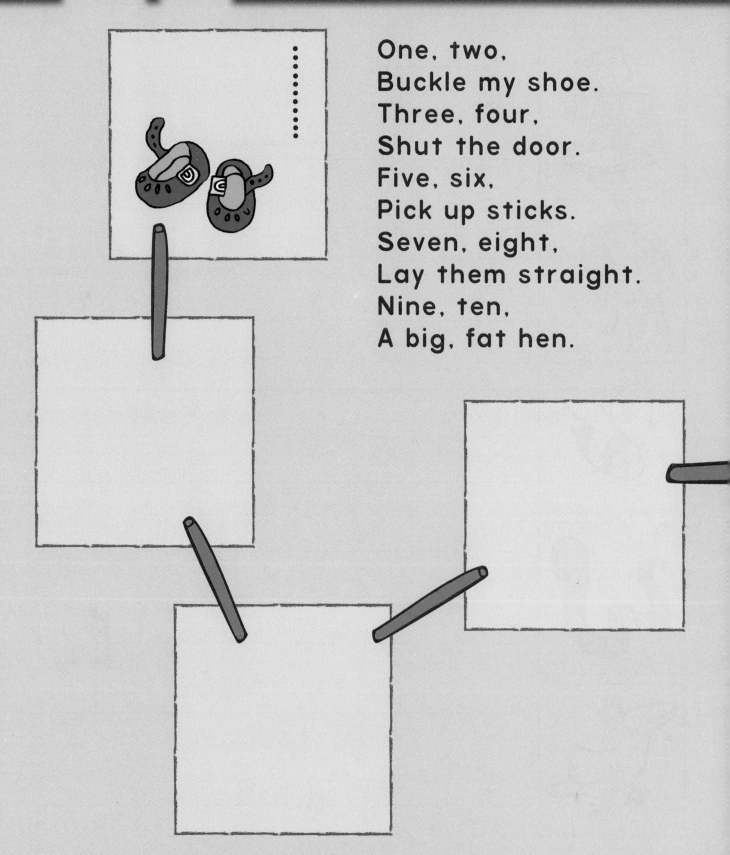

One, two,
Buckle my shoe.
Three, four,
Shut the door.
Five, six,
Pick up sticks.
Seven, eight,
Lay them straight.
Nine, ten,
A big, fat hen.

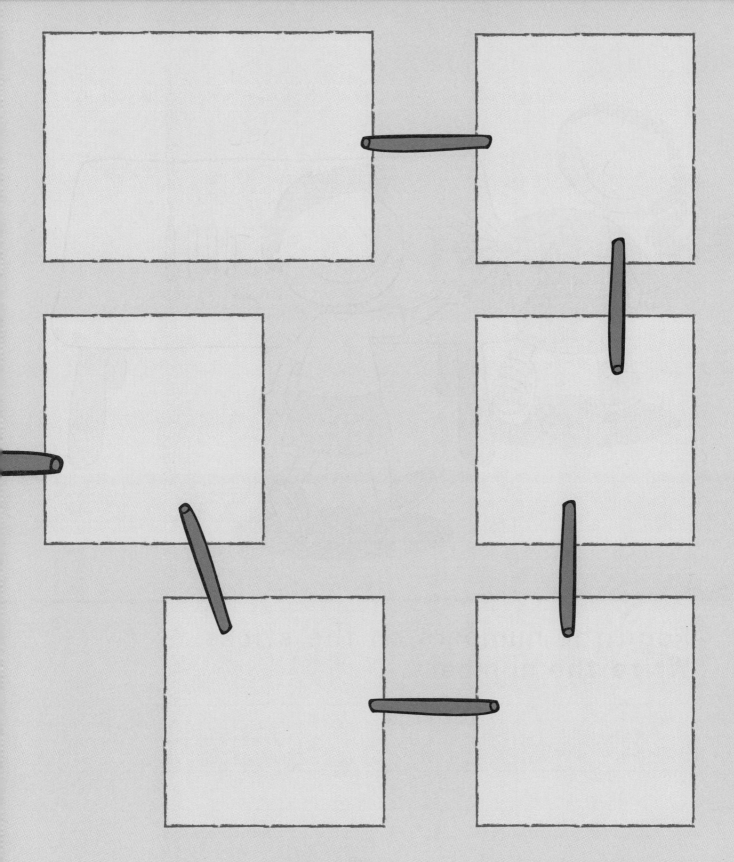

Activity

2

Collect the sticks.
Put them on the table.

Materials

Read the numbers on the sticks.
Write the numbers.

Put the sticks in order.

Write the numbers.

The numbers are in order.
Fill in the missing numbers.

The numbers are in order.
Fill in the missing numbers.

The numbers are in order.
Fill in the missing numbers.

1 Find ⬤ or ▭ in each picture.
Color the shape.

2

Find ▢ or ▭ in each picture.
Color the shape.

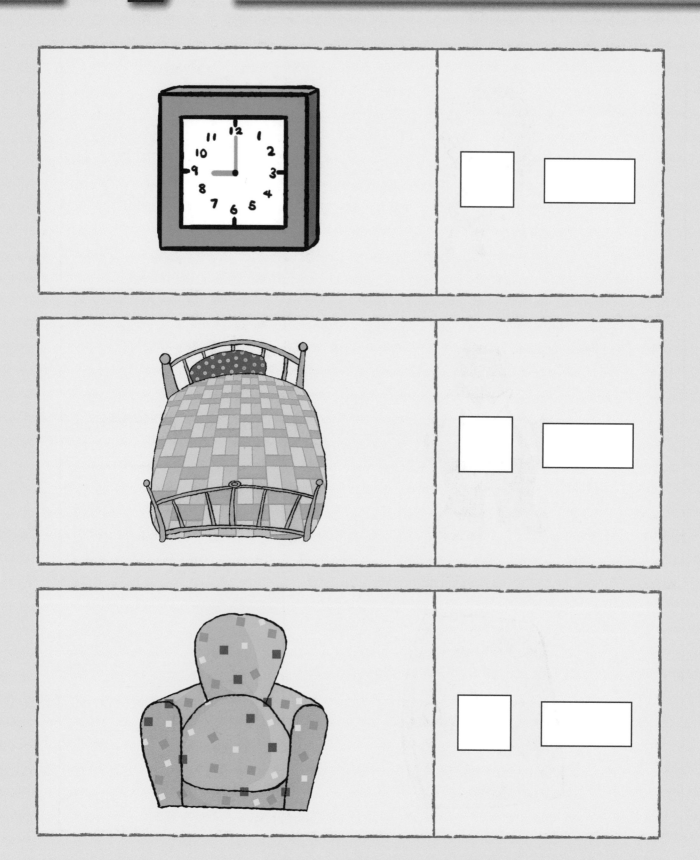

3

Find ☐ or △ in each picture.
Color the shape.

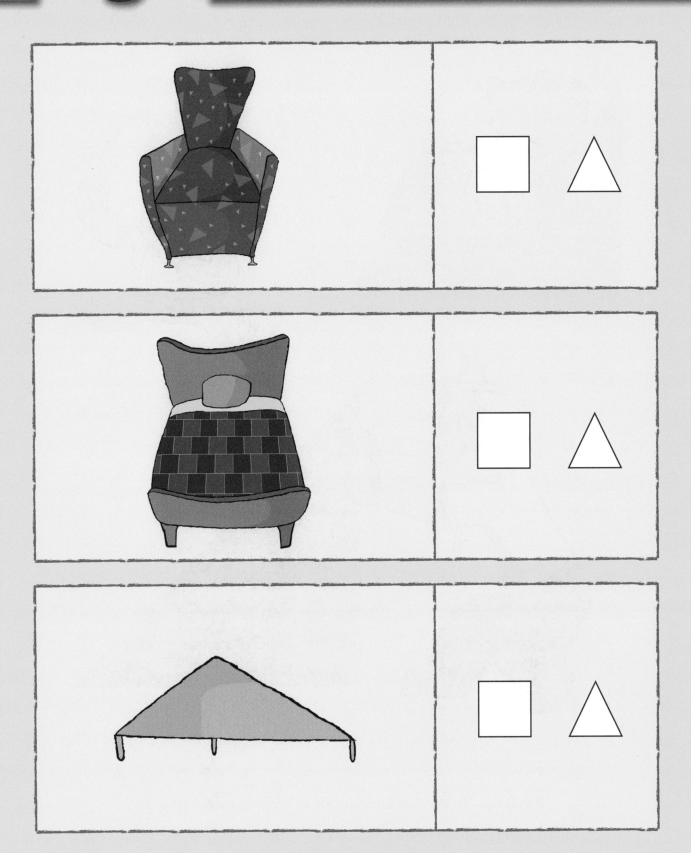

Cutouts: Page 99

Note: Have the students use the cutouts to form each of the shapes on pages 36 to 38. For the triangles on this page, have them record down the number of cutout pieces needed for each triangle.

How many pieces make the triangles?
Write the numbers.

 **piece makes**

Baby Bear's triangle.

 **pieces make**

Mama Bear's triangle.

 **pieces make**

Papa Bear's triangle.

Form this triangle using the cutouts.

Form this square using the cutouts.

Find 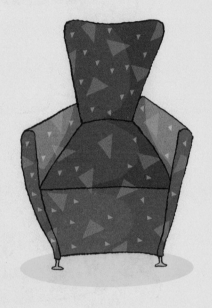 in the Three Bears' house.

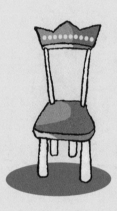

Find ◯▢▭△ in the Three Bears' house.

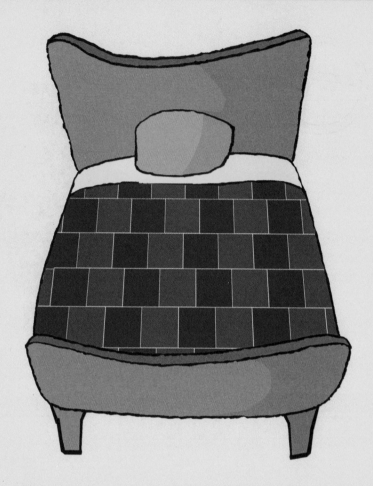

40

The Three Bears go on a treasure hunt ...

42

Count the ◯ ◻ ▬ △.
Write the numbers.

The Three Bears go on a trail.
Find ●■▬▬▲ in the map.

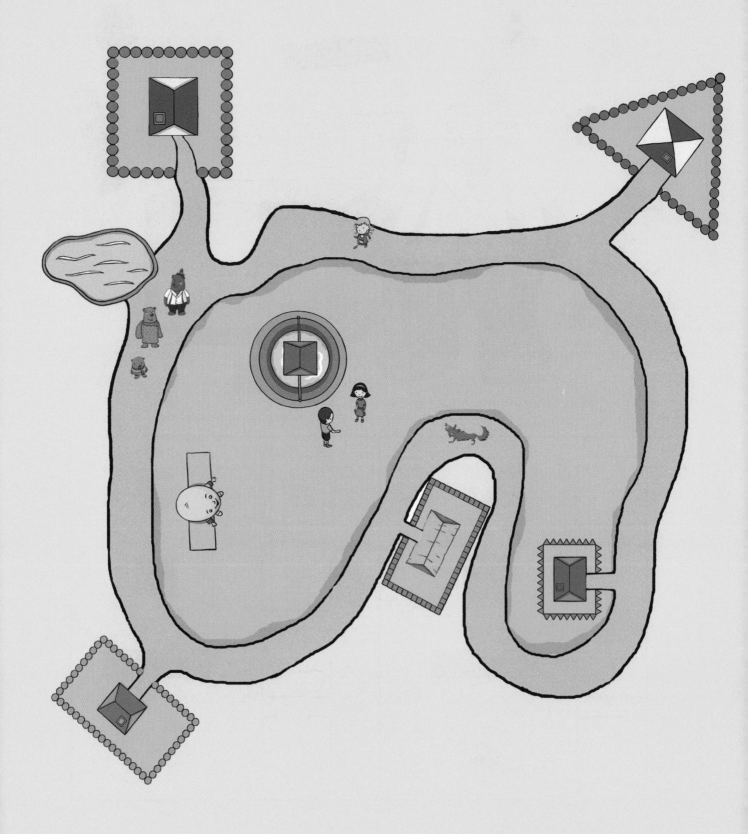

Along the way, the Three Bears meet ...
Find ⬤ ▢ ▭ △ in the pictures.

Help Tortoise find his way!
Look for the pattern ●●●●●●●.

Help Hare find his way!
Look for the pattern ●▲▲▲●▲▲.

Help Hare find his way!
Look for the pattern ■ ▪ ▪ ■ ▪ ■ ▪ ■.

Decorate the invitation card to the race.

Cutouts: Page 101

An Invitation to
the Race
Between

 and

5

Paste the next card in each pattern.

Cutouts: Page 103

Circle the next flag in each pattern.

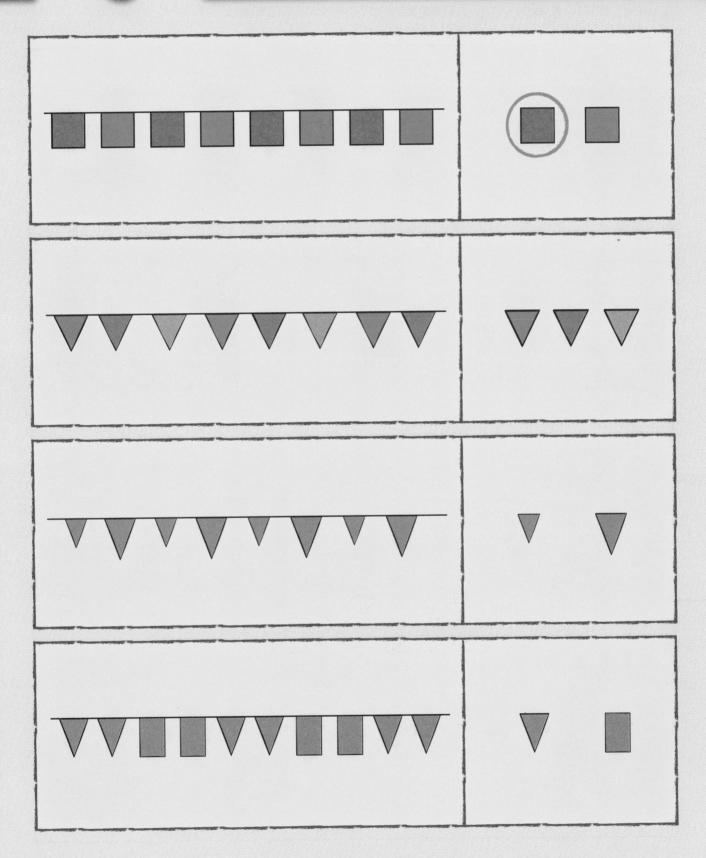

Circle the next flag in each pattern.

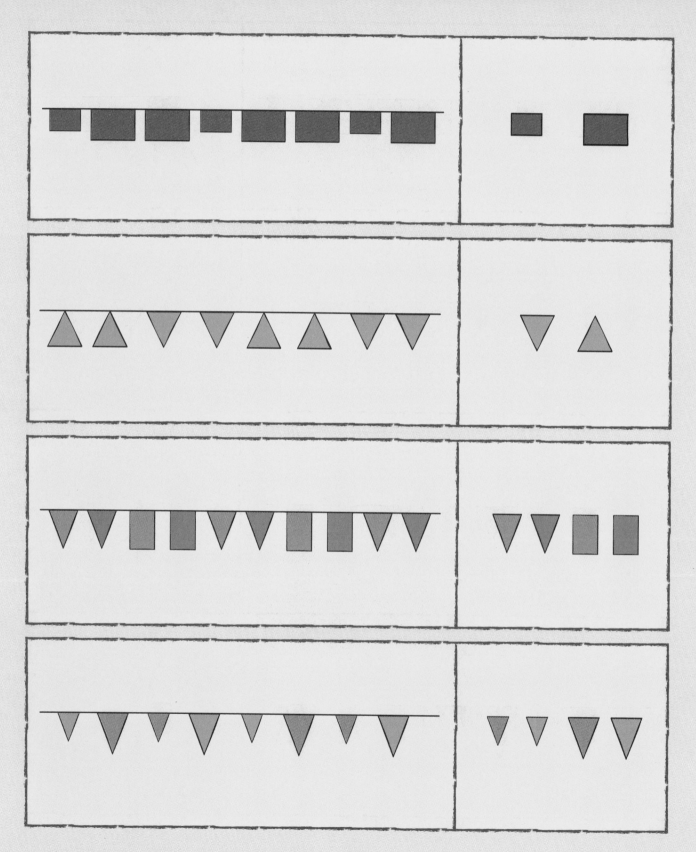

Talk about the pattern below each tree.

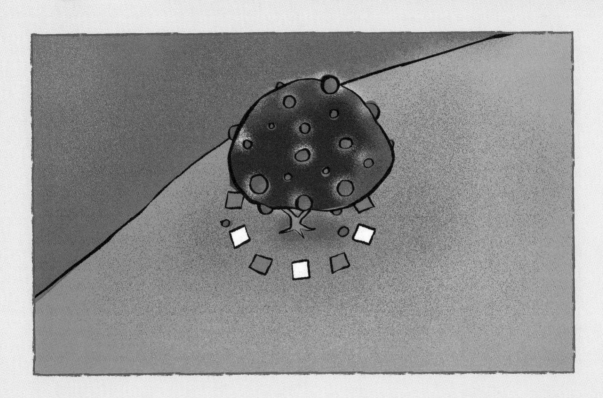

Talk about the pattern below each tree.

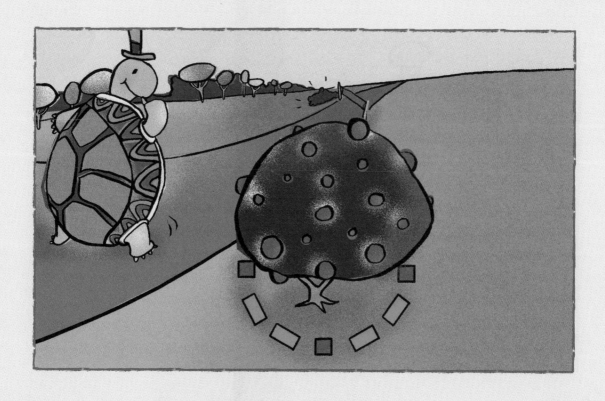

Talk about the pattern below each tree.

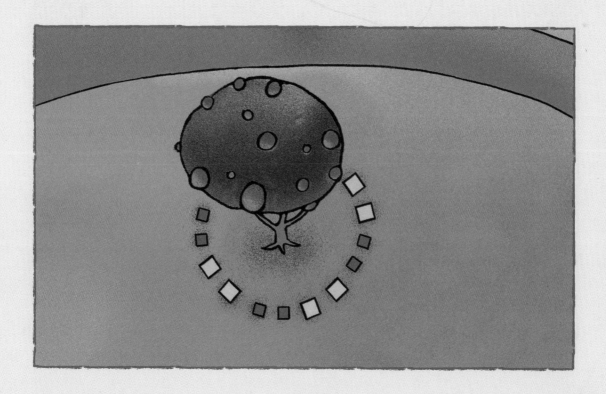

1 Measure the height and length. Write the numbers.

Cutouts: Page 105

5 🥄 tall

4 🥄 tall

2 🥄 tall

Measure the height and length.
Write the numbers.

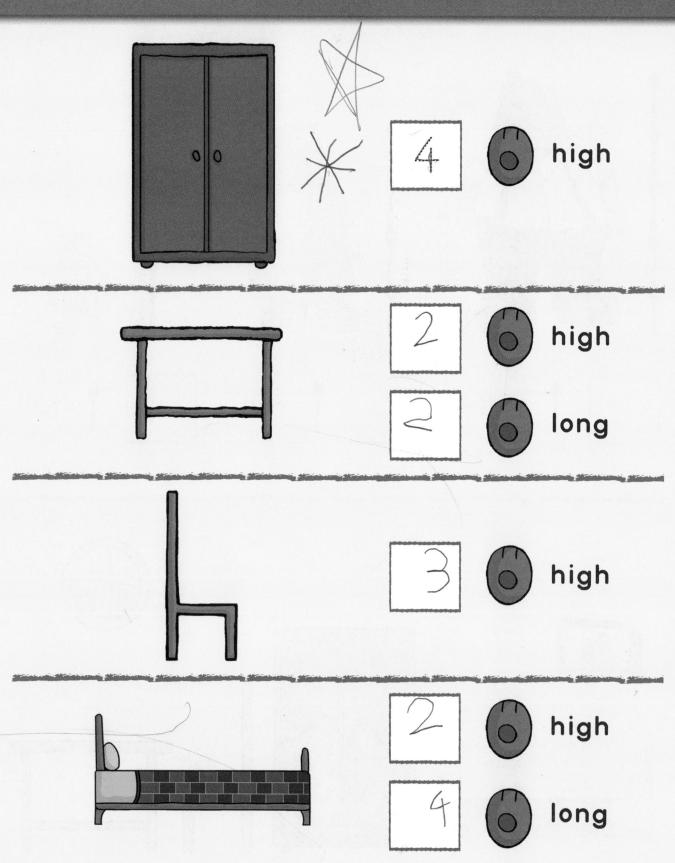

4 high

2 high

2 long

3 high

2 high

4 long

short
(tall)

(short)
tall

(short)
tall

short
(long)

(short)
long

Circle the correct word for each picture.

short

long

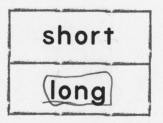

short

long

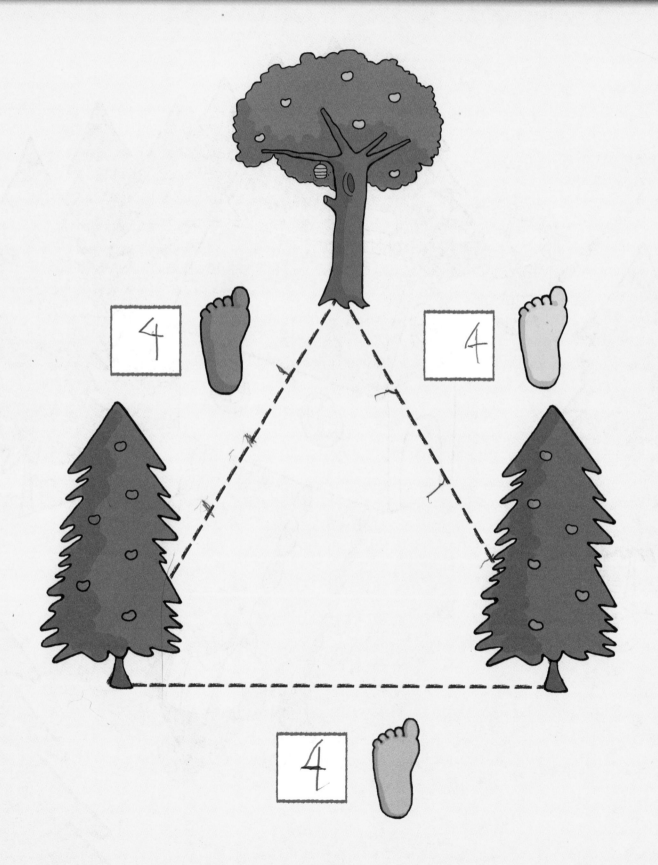

Who is taller?
Check (✔) the box.

Cutouts: Page 105

5 Put the cutouts in order.

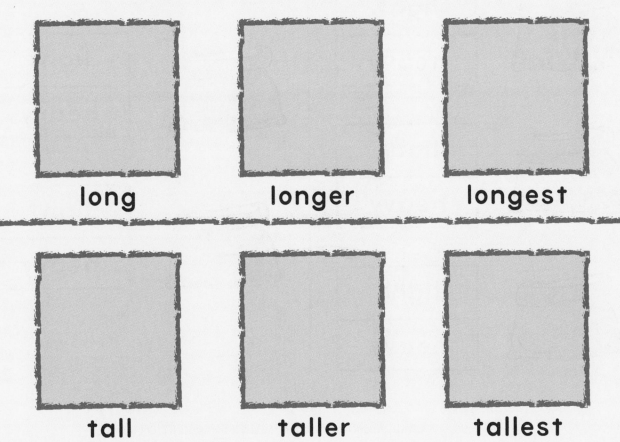

long   **longer**   **longest**

tall   **taller**   **tallest**

1

Carry the bags.
Circle the words.

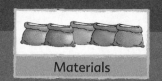

Materials

| light |
| heavy |

| light |
| heavy |

| light |
| heavy |

| light |
| heavy |

| light |
| heavy |

Note: Ask the students to lift each of the bags and say if the bag is light or heavy.

 is heavier.

 is heavier.

 is heavier.

Which is lighter?
Circle the face.

 is lighter.

 is lighter.

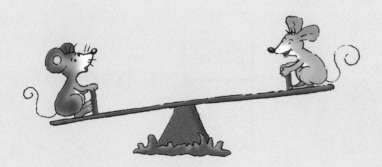

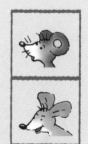 is lighter.

Activity

3

Which is heavier? Which is lighter?
Color the mice.

 is heavier than .

 is lighter than .

Which mouse is blue? Which mouse is green?

Which is heavier? Which is lighter?
Color the mice.

 is heavier than .

 is lighter than .

Which mouse is green? Which mouse is gray?

70

Make a mouse that is as heavy as 10 cubes.

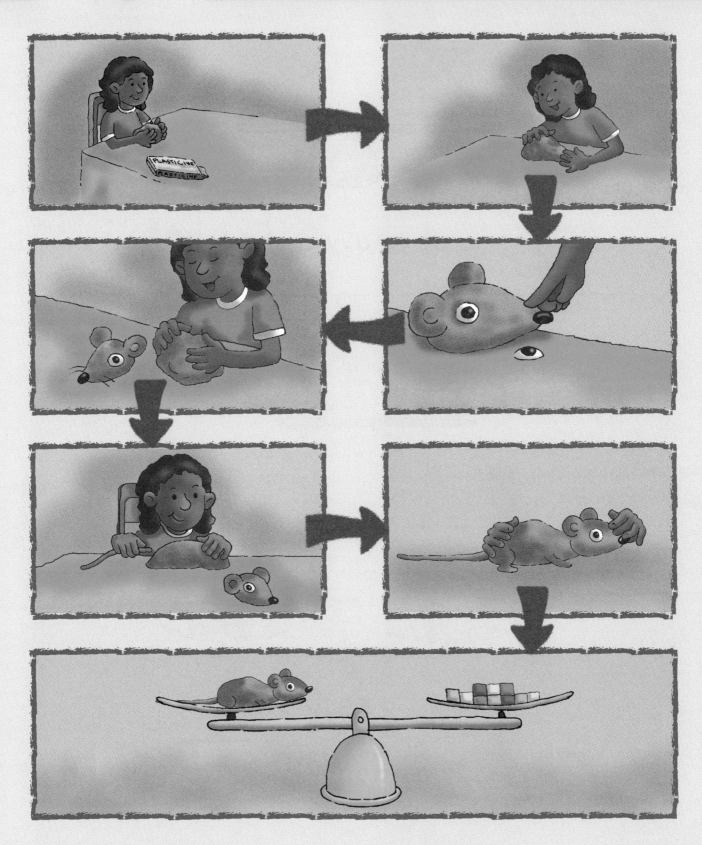

 is as heavy as 3 .

 is as heavy as [ ] .

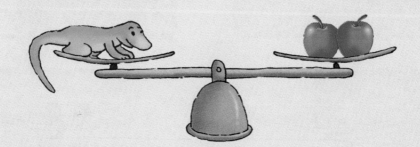

 is as heavy as [ ] .

72

How heavy is the clock?
Write the numbers.

 is as heavy as  .

 is as heavy as  .

 is as heavy as .

1

Do the activity.
Which bucket can hold more water?

Do the activity.
Which bucket can hold more water?

Materials

Note: Prepare six buckets of different colors. The capacity of these buckets should look similar but must not be the same. This activity is a progression from the previous one, where the differences in the capacity of the buckets are obvious.

Activity

3

Do the activity.
Color the glasses. Write the numbers.

Materials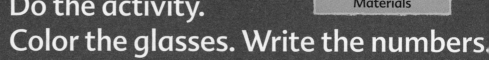

The can hold the same amount of

water as ☐ .

The can hold the same amount of

water as ☐ .

Do the activity.
Color the glasses. Write the numbers.

The 🪣 can hold the same amount of

water as ☐ 🥛.

The 🪣 can hold the same amount of

water as ☐ 🥛.

Activity

4

Do the activity.
Color the cups. Write the numbers.

Materials

The  can hold the same amount of

water as 10 .

___

The can hold the same amount of

water as 10 .

Do the activity.
Color the cups. Write the numbers.

The  can hold the same amount of

water as 10 cups.

___

The can hold the same amount of

water as 10 cups.

Now talk about the bucket.

Now talk about the bucket.

Which one can hold more water?

Which one can hold less water?

Which one can hold the most water?

Which one holds the least water?

1

Who has more?
Circle the face.

Cutouts: Pages 109 to 111

4

6

 has more  .

5

3

picked more .

Who has more?
Circle the face.

 has more $\bigcirc$.

 picked more $/$.

Which house has more?

Circle the house.

has more .

has more .

has more .

2

Which cup has
fewer sticks? Check (✔) the box.

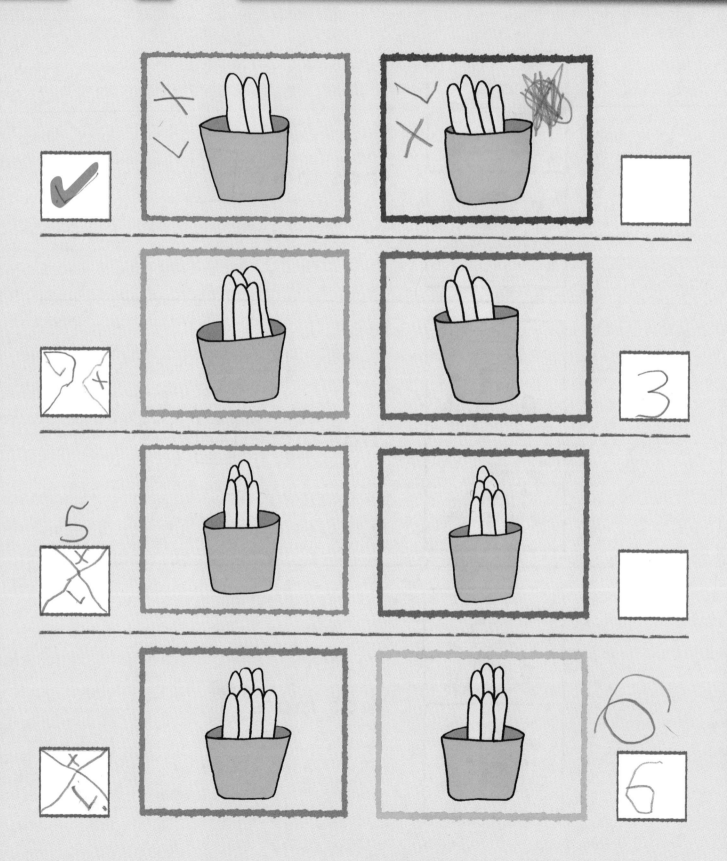

Which set has fewer?
Check (✔) the box.

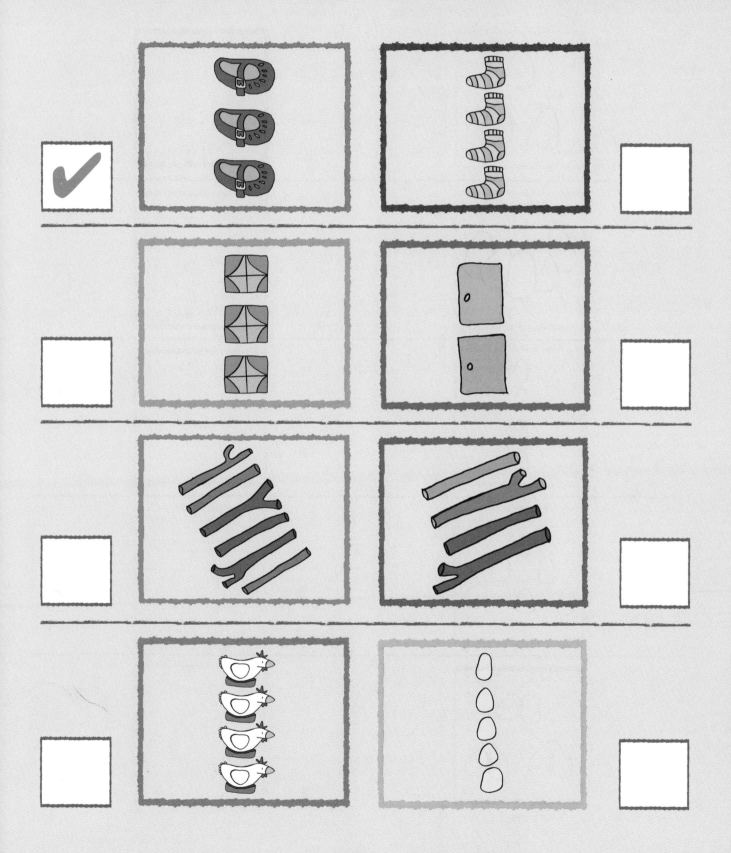

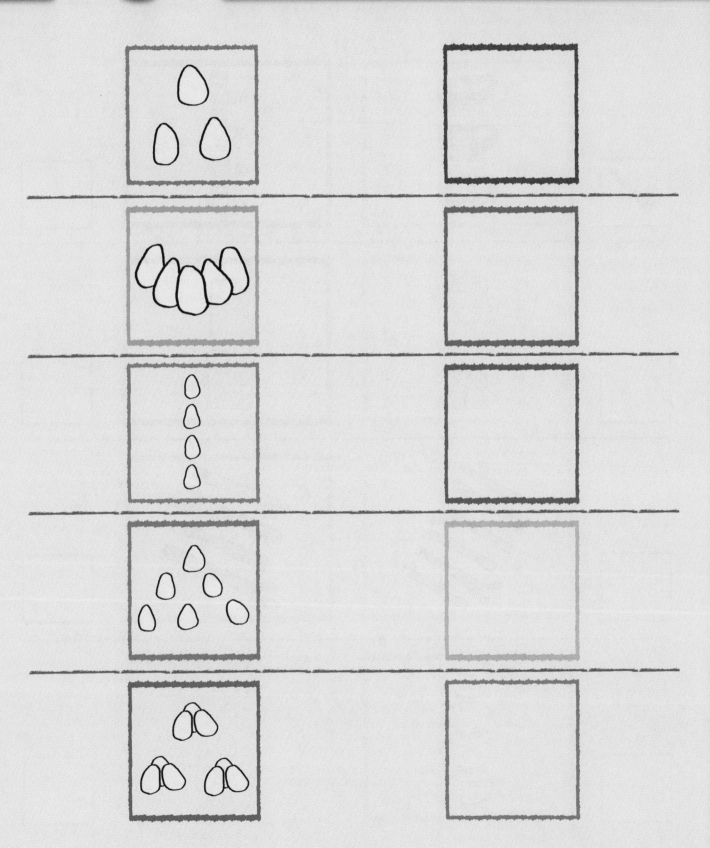

How many chicks are there?
Color the set with fewer chicks.

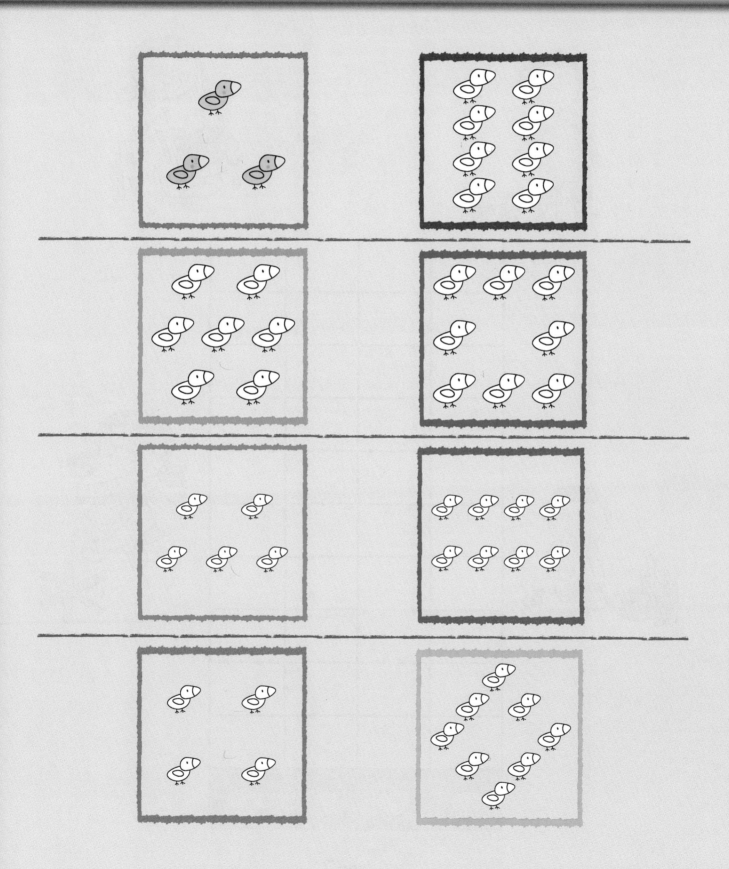

4

Count the sticks.
Paste the cutouts.

 Cutouts: Page 113

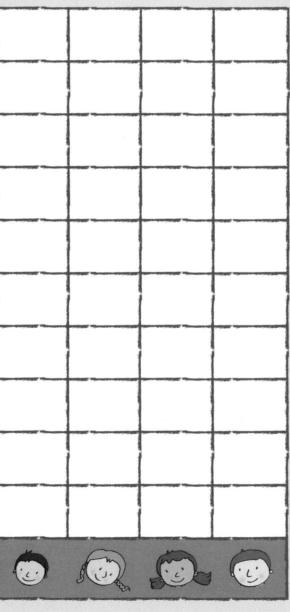

Who has more? Who has fewer?
Circle the face.

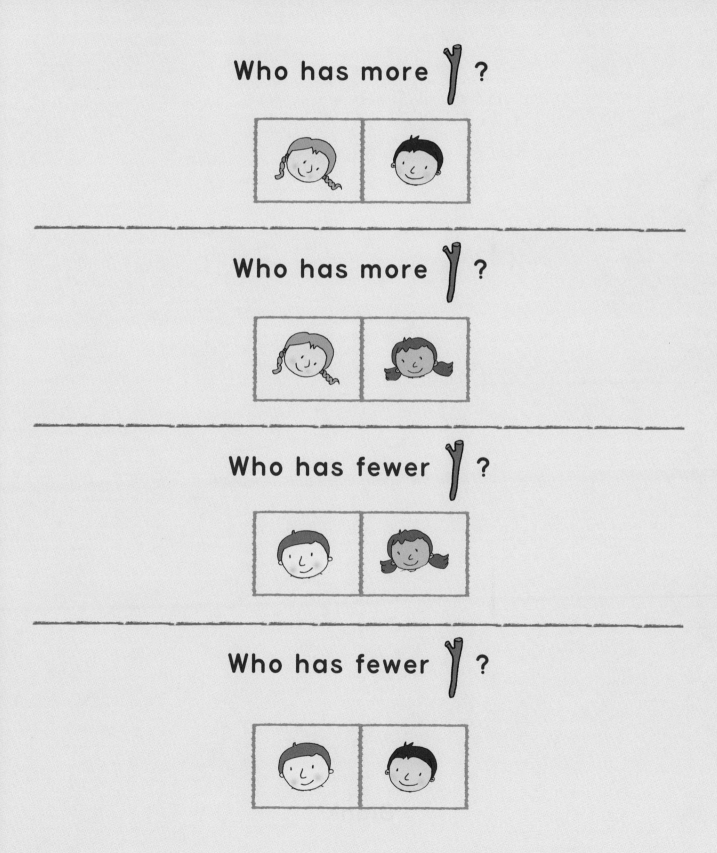

Who has more 𝗬 ?

Who has more 𝗬 ?

Who has fewer 𝗬 ?

Who has fewer 𝗬 ?

Blank

Cutouts for pages 26 and 27

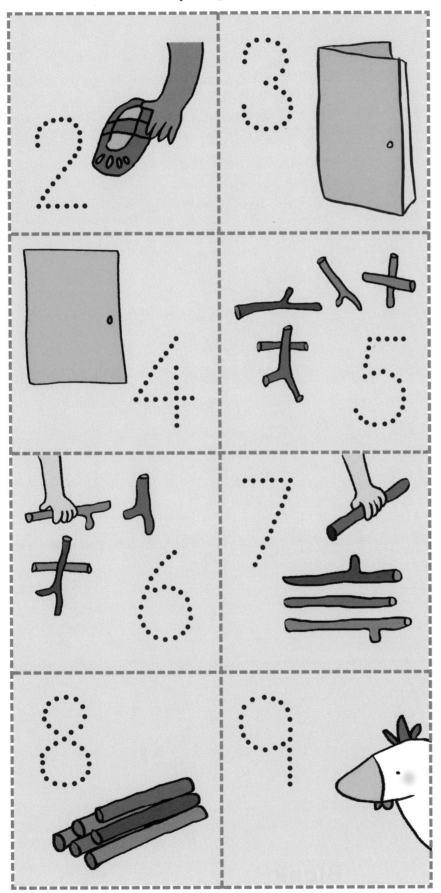

Blank

Cutouts for pages 26 and 27 (continued)

Cutouts for pages 36 to 38

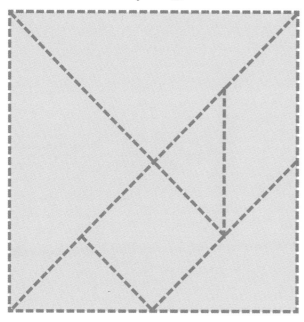

Blank

Cutouts for page 49

Blank

Cutouts for page 50

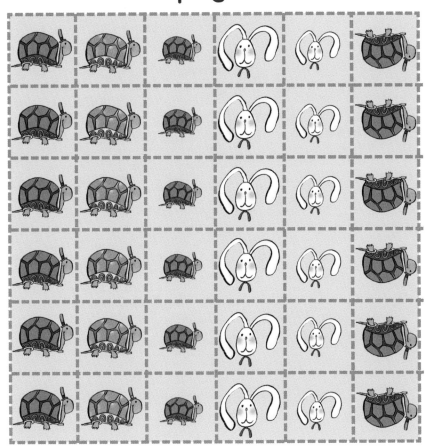

Blank

Cutouts for pages 57 and 58

Cutouts for page 65

Blank

Cutouts for page 81

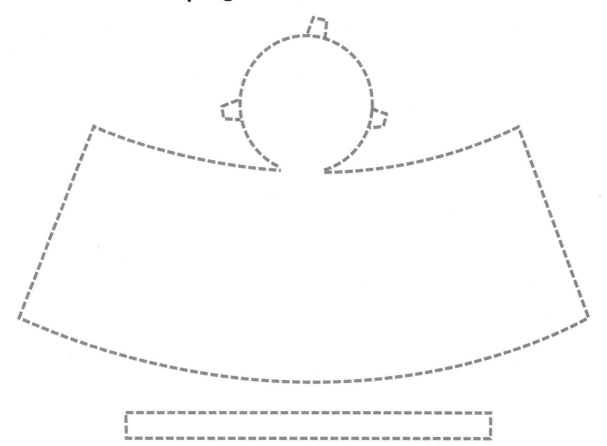

Blank

Cutouts for pages 82 to 85

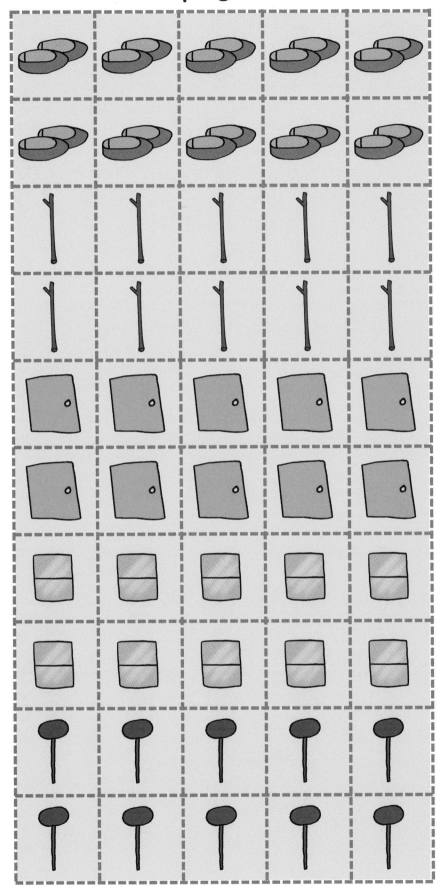

Blank

Cutouts for pages 82 to 85 (continued)

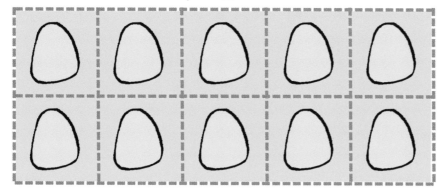

Cutouts for page 88

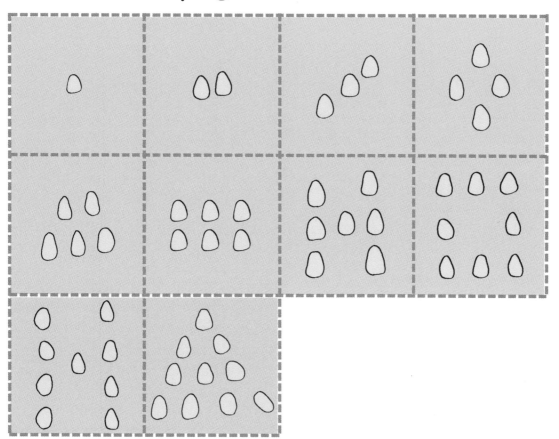

Blank

Cutouts for pages 90 and 91

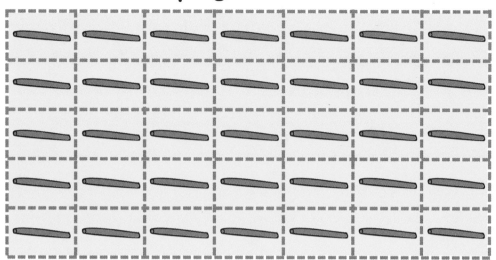

Blank